A Vermont Christmas

Photographs by Richard Brown

Text by Jay Parini

Best wishes

Richard Brown

Little, Brown and Company

Boston Toronto

First Edition

"Christmas 1945" from *A Matter of Fifty Houses* by Walter Hard.
Copyright 1952 by Walter Hard. Reprinted by permission of
Vermont Books: Publishers, Middlebury, VT.

"Champlain in Winter" from *Orrery* by Richard Kenney.
Copyright © 1985 by Richard Kenney. Reprinted with the permission
of Atheneum Publishers, an imprint of Macmillan Publishing
Company.

"Ice Fishing" from *Anthracite Country* by Jay Parini. Copyright © 1982
by Jay Parini. Reprinted with the permission of the author.

"Good-by and Keep Cold" from *The Poetry of Robert Frost* edited by
Edward Connery Lathem. Copyright 1923 by Holt, Rinehart and
Winston, Inc. and renewed 1951 by Robert Frost. Reprinted by
permission of Henry Holt and Company, Inc.

Library of Congress Cataloging-in-Publication Data
Brown, Richard, 1945–
A Vermont Christmas.

1. Vermont – Description and travel – 1981– – Views.
2. Christmas – Vermont – Pictorial works.
3. Vermont – Social life and customs – Pictorial works.
I. Parini, Jay.   II. Title.
F50.B76   1988   974.3 043   88–12707
ISBN 0–316–11075–2

10 9 8 7 6 5 4 3 2 1

Published simultaneously in Canada by
Little, Brown & Company (Canada) Limited

Printed in the United States of America

A Vermont Christmas

Introduction

"People come here from around the country to see what Christmas ought to look like," says Marsh Franklin, a farmer near Ludlow. "They expect snow – lots of snow – and big pine trees. They want towns that look like something from an old book, with a general store and a village green. They want little white churches with sharp steeples and court-houses with cement pillars stuck up front. And they want to walk into a corner drugstore and sit at the soda fountain and catch a bit of gossip about how the Congregational choir has gone to wrack and ruin since so-and-so took over. They may hope for a sleigh ride, too. People are funny about sleigh rides. I guess that's why they all want to spend Christmas in Vermont."

Vermont, by reason, ought to have no special claims on Christmas. But over the years, the image of Vermont has cast its spell on the nation's consciousness. Perhaps Currier and Ives are to blame. During the middle of the last century, their lithographs of country life at Christmas featured imagery of horse-drawn sleighs and piny woods filled with snow; these famous drawings imprinted on the American mind a particular idea of Christmas – an idea that has stuck. Today, whether Christmas arrives over the Louisiana bayou or in the midst of an Arizona desert, children still imagine Santa on his sleigh, with a host of reindeer pawing the snow on the roof of a little house in a quaint village that looks something like Vermont.

Vermont is, more than anything else, a state of mind. Cross the neighboring borders into New York, New Hampshire, Massachusetts, or Canada, and you lose the magic. It makes no rational sense, but since when does logic matter where sentiment is at stake? Vermont, with the Green Mountains careering down its spine, with its rolling pastureland and postcard villages, has a geographical identity all its own, an identity that seems to shift admirably with the seasons but to culminate on the twenty-fifth of December.

The spring here is called "mud season," and it seems a long way from Christmas. As the snows melt and the land thaws, it's as if the earth beneath your feet turns to water. The streams and creeks (even a river is usually called a "creek" in the world of New England under-statement) gurgle and swell. Meanwhile, sap trickles down the maple trunks, and dozens of sleepy animals stagger out of hibernation into the crisp air. Toward late spring, the cherry and apple blossoms sign the air with their powerful scents and colors.

Summer is heaven in these parts, a time when Vermont becomes Old England. Maple trees grow thick, while thin popples dangle their wrists like their cousins, the western aspens. Birches shimmer. Everywhere, white pine and spruce and balsam fir bush out. There is plenty of open, green pastureland, too, all nicely contained, thoroughly *human*, unlike the (perhaps) frightening prairies or deserts found elsewhere in the United States. "Vermont is kind of cozy," Mr. Franklin says. "People feel safe here – bounded."

The fall is, of course, famous in Vermont. The hillsides become a crazy quilt of light, and tourists from all over the country come to observe the gaudy display. They're called "leaf peepers," and the local radio stations offer them daily reports on the progress of the color, although the announcers are as duly tentative as weathermen, knowing that a sudden dip in the temperature or a windy patch can change the picture overnight.

Winter comes early to Vermont. (Some say it never leaves.) And with winter comes the thought of Christmas. Soon after Thanksgiving, the towns put up their lights and decorations. The shop windows become a dazzle of red ribbons and green crepe. And one sees manger scenes in front of churches or in drugstore windows. It is the rare December that doesn't bring with it tons of snow, transforming the normally complex countryside into an ethereal sameness – white on white – as the smell of burning logs tinges the air.

This book is about Christmas and its season in Vermont. The photographs, by Richard Brown, invoke many familiar and some unfamiliar images of this state in winter. Town life and country life are both represented, the human landscape blending with the wild. As William Blake, the poet, once said, "Without man, nature is barren." The nature found in these photographs is anything but barren. It is perpetually caught and transmogrified by the human eye, *naturalized*, as it were, and made habitable by the imagination.

The text is written to complement the photographs, to invoke the sense of what it means and has meant to live in Vermont during the Christmas season. Some unique Vermont traditions are recalled, and some Vermonters are allowed to speak for themselves, including a fair number of Vermont writers, from Robert Frost to Richard Kenney. There is a lot of history here, too: natural history as well as human history.

Some of the readings in this book are designed for active use on Christmas Eve as children gather about their parents' ankles to listen to poems or stories while the wood stove blazes and the Christmas tree shines. (A few selections are more obviously for adults, who may prefer to read them to themselves after the children have gone to bed!) *The Light at Scromfit House*, a Christmas tale for children, was written specifically for this volume.   J.P.

13

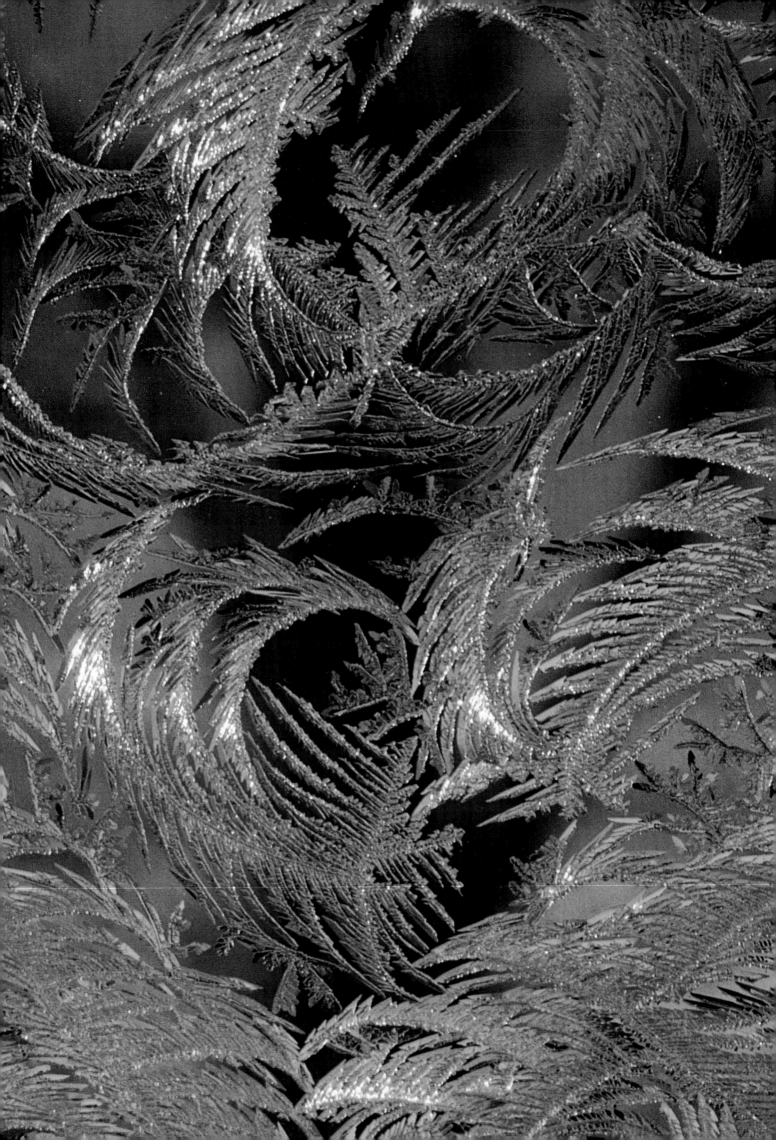

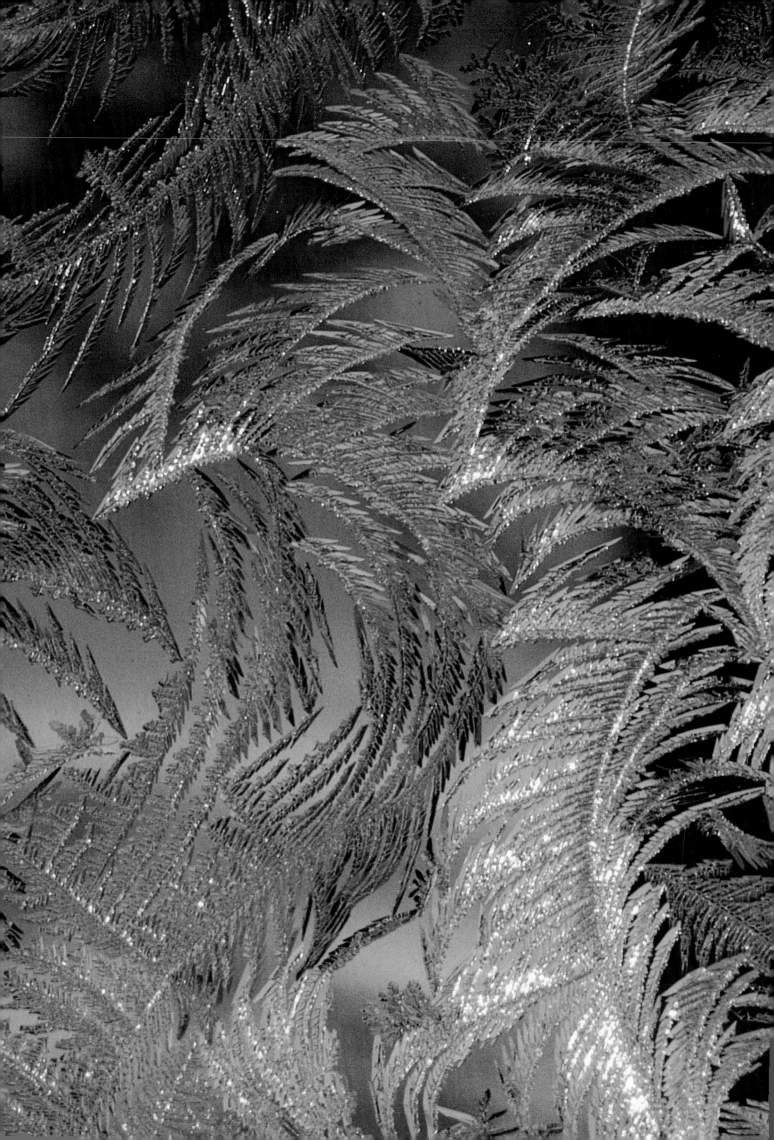

Luminaria

Christmas is a time for lights, for what the villagers of West Dummerston (population six hundred) call *luminaria*. According to the dictionary, luminaria means "illuminations betokening rejoicing." Perhaps because so many of Vermont's old towns center on a village green, a concentration of lighting effects can make a difference. There's nothing quite like driving through Goshen, Chelsea, Calais, or West Dummerston on Christmas Eve, when the white clapboard houses, most dating back to the last century or before, shimmer with a single candle in each window.

Electric lights just aren't the same thing, as Mary Brooks realized in 1974, when she returned from a spell in New York State, where the little town of DeWitt had a local tradition that caught her attention. DeWitt's fire department would set out along the roadside little white bags with candles in them. On Christmas Eve, they would light the candles. When Mary returned to West Dummerston, her native town, she decided to import this tradition – and it has stuck.

That first year, she and her friends at the local Baptist Church somewhat sparsely lined the main street of the town with eighty-five bags. The white, waxed bakery bags contained a few inches of road sand and a single plumber's candle. The bags were spaced about ten paces apart and were lit for two evenings before Christmas and on Christmas night itself. The effect was startling, creating a soft glow announcing to the world: "Make way for the Christ child!" Now, instead of merely eighty-five candles in bags, the town can boast over three hundred. To insure the continuance of this tradition, the Baptist Church has established a Luminaria Committee, and there seems to be no lack of interest.

The tradition of lighting up one's town in this particular way can be traced to Mexico, where part of that country's famous *Navidad* involves setting out candles in brown paper bags along the roadways, even along the rooftops, to celebrate the birth of Christ. The candles are lit on Christmas Eve, when the Mexicans enact a symbolic walk through their neighborhoods, retracing the steps of Mary and Joseph as they searched, without success, for a room for the night. The quest usually ends at the home of a friend, where food and drink is waiting, and the celebration continues far into the night.

In West Dummerston, the candles are lit on Christmas Eve at six o'clock, lighting the way for carolers, who proceed from house to house with flashlights on hymnals. The candles are put out at nine, to save what's left of their light for the next evening. On Christmas itself, after dark, the candles are lit for the last time and allowed to burn out, one by one. "We feel kind of proud of these lights," says one villager. "People drive over from neighboring towns to see them. They know Christmas means a lot to the people of West Dummerston."

Of course electric lights still brighten many, if not most, landmark towns in Vermont, some of which take special pride in their displays. Burlington, St. Johnsbury, and Rutland are always well lit during the holiday season. But Vergennes, near Lake Champlain, has long been the Christmas dandy of Vermont towns, attracting gawkers from all over the state to its shimmering Main Street and village green.

Vergennes's pride goes back a long way. In the last century, steamers going southwest through the Champlain Canal and north to Canada used to call in Vergennes, which had splendid accommodations at the Stevens House – a glorious structure, still in use, built in the late 1700s. A tourist in Vergennes in 1819, Levi Woodbury (later a U.S. Supreme Court Justice) observed in his diary that the dress and manners of the local population "seem much more like a Seaport than those in Rutland or Middlebury." He found well-dressed men smoking big cigars, ladies in calico, and a passion for elegance in the homes and public houses. Though Vergennes is not so prosperous as it once was, the elegant houses are beautifully maintained, and the town's main street, a monument to redbrick architecture, is bedecked with brightly colored lights from the week after Thanksgiving through the first week of the New Year. J.P.

The Church as Meeting House

Christmas Eve services take place all over the state, often in little churches of such exquisite clarity and grace that one regrets the impossibility of being in more than one place at one time.

Churches often form a kind of centerpiece for the Vermont townscape, places of worship and community life. The long tradition of town meetings – a cornerstone of democracy in New England – could almost not have happened without these little churches, which provided a familiar, convenient gathering spot where local farmers could meet with townsfolk to settle their differences and make plans for their communal future. A fine example of this meeting of secular and sacred is the United Church of Strafford, which dominates the green of this classic village. "I've been going to town meeting in that church for sixty years," says Jim Weatherall, a dairy farmer whose family has lived in the

Strafford region for over a century and a half. "Made more enemies there than I can count. Every time I look at that building, my blood boils."

The village of Chelsea, the county seat of Orange County, is among the most beautiful in Vermont. Its Greek revival courthouse, built in 1847, is impressively well proportioned and stately. But the Chelsea West Hill Union Meeting House, built fourteen years earlier, is just as fine, though more severe. It originally contained only fifty-two pews, all facing the front door – an arrangement altered when the Meeting House was expanded and remodeled in 1902. Six different denominations shared the same building, which was also used for town meetings.

The atmosphere in the West Hill Meeting House, now called the West Hill Church, is one of starkness. The church reeks of northernness and winter, of hardship and isolation. The backs of the pews are perpendicular, forming a perfect right angle with the seats – a suitable design for those who still want to practice the harsher forms of Puritanism. "Never were seats constructed with a more sublime unconsciousness of the anatomy of the human frame," says a local preacher, the Reverend Francis Hemenway.

The West Hill Church is heated by wood, as it always has been. (A second wood stove was added in 1853 – a concession to the less spiritually rigorous members of the congregation.) To get enough wood to last through the Vermont winters, the church holds a woodcutting bee every few years on a hot summer weekend. "It's kind of hard to get excited about wood stoves in July," says one of the church's current members. "And you always think you cut too much. But winter up here is serious business. If I didn't know better, I'd say it gets colder every year." George Bradshaw, a local farmer, thinks so, too – and he should know. He's the man who arrives at the West Hill Church several hours before the rest of the congregation to stoke the fires on those bitter Sunday mornings between Christmas and Easter.

St. Stephen's on the Green, the Episcopal church in Middlebury, is a landmark, too. Its Christmas Eve service attracts hundreds of parishioners and visitors. The rector of St. Stephen's, the Reverend Addison Hall, recently showed me a letter written on December 31, 1871, by a parishioner named Homer Sheldon. It recreates the aura of Christmas traditions in this ancient parish:

> It is Sunday evening of a rainy, slippery, icy, time. Let me tell you
> about our Christmas Tree at St. Stephen's Church. First, Mr. Lord
> and Byron Fleming went to Ripton and got a spruce larger than a stove
> pipe and so high that it touched the ceiling overhead inside the chancel.

It stood inside a cask and was surrounded by bricks and rigged with ropes like a ship's mainmast. The exhibition was Thursday, and I went in and found the tree burning with nearly a hundred candles. The tree was hung full of large red apples, too. There must have been a hundred little packages of every description hanging from its branches: books, pictures, popcorn candies, and every variety of articles suitable for one's friends. After a few prayers, the Sunday Scholars advanced up each aisle, singing in procession, up to the chancel there after a few carols. The Rev. Mr. Lord called out the names on the gifts, and the people came forward and received the presents and retired. It took about an hour to relieve the tree of all those presents. After a few remarks by Mr. Lord and singing a few more carols, the services were ended by singing the old Gloria in Excelsis by the choir in its white robes, and thus ended a very pleasant and joyous meeting for all who attended. I was much pleased with the whole thing. My wife and Maria both being sick with colds did not dare venture out, of course. You know what winter is like up here. In any case, we had a good old-fashioned Christmas Eve, even though so many faces are gone from choir, which is not what it used to be.

It must be the rare choir indeed that is really "what it used to be." Nevertheless, Mr. Sheldon's letter suggests an immense spirit of community, a point reinforced by Phil Fitzpatrick, a lawyer who belongs to the Second Congregational Church in Hyde Park, a little town southeast of Burlington. "Christmas in Vermont is a time of community. It's a time when people think about the poor, the sick, and the elderly. Nobody gets forgotten," he says.

For Mr. Fitzpatrick, the high point of the season is the candlelight service in his church on Christmas Eve. "The service is basically a time for singing the traditional carols. We've been practicing for several nights, going door to door in the snow throughout the village. That's all preparation for Christmas Eve – a lovely service that ends when all the lights are extinguished and a single candle flame is lit. The flame is passed from person to person, until the whole church is lit up. It's very moving."

"The message of Christmas is simple," says the Reverend Sharon Lloyd of Middlebury. "It says that hope has come into the world."

J.P.

Champlain in Winter

Richard Kenney

Kenney, born in 1948, has lived, off and on, in Vermont through much of his life. One of America's best younger poets, he has won numerous prizes, including the coveted MacArthur Fellowship. His most recent collection of poems, Orrery, chronicles a year on a Vermont farm.

Deep winter, crossing Lake Champlain. Here
the north wind is steadier than gravity;
it has a long sweep down from Canada
before it intersects the Grande Isle causeway.
Sawteeth: icicles all horizontal
off the guardrail cables— compass points,
each bearing south across the grey expanse,
where two linked forms unfrozen in the windsock
of the fog and telescoping whorl
of snow and scarcely visible at all
can just be brought to focus: *skidding deer
on crazed ice; light dog loping.*

Ice Fishing

Jay Parini

This poem is from Parini's volume of poetry, Anthracite Country, published in 1982.

The snow ticks off my cheeks, I raise my eyes,
and flakes like houseflies buzz against my gaze.
The ice squeaks underfoot as I go out
to fish on Hatchet Pond through frozen gauze.

The day whites out whichever way I look.
Big hemlocks ring the pond, their branches light
as dove wings, drooping feathers to the ground.
The blank eye hates this poverty of sight

and digs. I chip away the month of freeze
and splinter with an ax the ice that grows
like cancer inward from a whitish skin.
The minnows fly like sparks beneath my blows.

The taphole plunges like a wrist through ice,
then water breaks in ringlets of blue frost.
I drop a line along it back to summer,
fishing inside myself for what I've lost.

Rita Bumps
Remembers Christmas

The following recollection is based on a series of interviews with Rita Bumps, who now lives in Middlebury. She grew up on a typical farm in eastern Vermont during the 1920s and 1930s.

The best Christmases seem to be the ones a long time ago. We lived on a farm down near East Barnard, not far from Woodstock, with my mother and father, me, and fourteen brothers and sisters. That was a big family, sure, and we were poor enough. But you never *knew* you were poor in those days, since you had all you wanted: plenty to eat, a warm bed, a house. And when Christmas came, you were so happy. You'd been waiting for that day all year long.

Those years were the happiest on record, a period they now call the Depression. It was back in the late twenties and early thirties, before you had so many cars or money you could spend. We made our own fun, playing in the snow, listening to stories around the wood stove. Truth is, there was so much work to be done, you didn't think about it. Your mind was full of what had to be done, and there was always something: a cow to be milked, a fence to mend, a loaf of bread to be kneaded, or a small child to wash and dress. You just went about your business.

All through the fall we were getting ready for Christmas. For the women, there was plenty of knitting to do: our mittens and sweaters, caps – all homemade, with the wool boiled so the knit was close and water couldn't seep through so easy. It seemed like the Christmas cooking went on for months, too, since every time you made a fresh batch of maple Christmas cookies you ate it, which left you back to square one.

Starting in October, you watched every day for the postman, Mr. Forrest, knowing that sooner or later those packages would arrive from down south. We had a couple of old aunts who sent a box of things for the family each year like clockwork, what you might call luxuries: nice underwear and socks, maybe some chocolates or perfume. Presents meant a lot to us, since we didn't get much the rest of the year.

I remember my grandfather sitting by the stove with that penknife of his, whittling away like his life depended on it. He'd make all sorts of odd things that would turn up later in your Christmas stocking: a whistle, or a figurine. He was, by profession, what you might call an old Yankee horse trader, since you traded horses in those days like they do cars now. He traveled up and down the valley, calling at farms, dickering like an Arab. My family was known everywhere as one that could dicker, but we learned it from him.

Horses got you where you wanted going in those days, which was before you got used to seeing cars. In summer, they were used to plough the fields, since most of us didn't have machine tractors yet. In winter, they pulled the sleighs. You didn't scrape the roads clean when it snowed, remember. You rolled them flat then, for the sleighs to slide on. We had a big old sleigh come down through the family, and one of our favorite days before Christmas was the day when my father took us shopping into South Royalton, half a dozen miles away. I think each of us had a quarter or fifty cents to spend, and we'd occupy ourselves for weeks with wondering what to buy, whether a spool of thread, a few pencils, or a paper kite. In our family, the girls didn't much care for dolls, since we had enough *real* babies to go round.

We'd pile into the sleigh, every kid big enough to walk, putting our feet on what we called a "free stone" – kind of like a gravestone – that my father had warmed at the stove. With that steaming below your soles, it didn't matter how cold it might drop. There was nothing like it, flying through the woods like that, with the horses blowing a white breath ahead of them. It felt like you were riding a magic carpet.

In town there was a general store where we bought provisions, like flour and salt, and things like frying pans. But there wasn't much needed beyond what we had on the farm already. We kept our own cows for milking. We had chickens for eggs and pigs for ham and bacon. We had an orchard, a small one, but it gave you apples that would last almost the year round in the root cellar. You had cider jelly, too, which you spread on homemade bread and ate for dessert most nights. I figure we raised enough vegetables and fruit during the summer months to keep us going through the whole year and then some. We canned everything from the usual beans to dandelion greens to milk-weeds, with their tender tops. Boy, were they ever good! Nowadays you pay a pretty penny for this kind of thing in a health food store – and it doesn't taste the half.

Mother was a cook renowned in those parts, and an expert with making things like cottage cheese and tapioca and butter. You never understood exactly when she'd be making that stuff. It seems she just kept a pan of milk on the back of the stove all the time, pouring off the whey when it was ready, sieving out the curds. You just took all that for granted, especially the taste. Food doesn't taste the same today, with all the chemicals they add.

Of course, there was maple syrup. Even in a bad year, when the sap didn't hardly run, you had plenty of that. Our sugar bush was one of the biggest in those parts, so we had plenty of syrup, which we used for everything. There was always a dish of it on the kitchen table – for oatmeal, for coffee. We used it for everything you could think of and some things you couldn't. It made wonderful fudge, combined with the hazelnuts we gathered from the woods. Hazelnut fudge was almost the best thing you could eat back then. Almost as good as syrup on snow, which was the finest treat in the world. And so easy! All you did was boil down the syrup till it got really nice and thick, then pour it straight onto fresh snow. It would harden so you could pick it up to lick, like a pane of candy glass.

There was always a pot of tea on the stove, too – for visitors. You never quite finished a pot of it without adding more grounds, which meant it was strong enough to wake the dead. A lot of people came by, especially around the holidays. You know what a farm town is like, with all the gossip and stories. Whether they were true or not didn't seem much to the point, and it was rude to question somebody about what they said. In the later years, we had a radio, but the programs never matched up to the local gossip. At night, we'd all sit around talking and playing a card game called King Pede (in which you had to make a score of one hundred) and drinking tea. I don't recall having had as much fun since.

When I was eight, a story happened that was true. It was almost Christmas, and I was working with my father in the barn, me and my younger brother. He was maybe seven, if that much. Well, my father got called off to another part of the farm, leaving us alone there. I don't know whose idea it was, but we decided to surprise him and butcher a cow. I picked out one that I knew was ready, since my father had mentioned it, and led her up to the part of the barn floor where the dirty work was done. She kind of tugged at the rope, like she didn't want to come. Cows are smart that way.

We drew straws to see who would get to shoot her, since that was the real fun. My brother won, so he took my father's gun from the rack and shot her right in the brain at close range. That did the trick. She looked at us kind of queer for a moment – at least I imagine she did – then fell hard on the dirt floor. We were tickled pink.

My job was to stick her in the throat, which I did, just above the breastbone like I'd seen it done a hundred times. I didn't hesitate a minute, following that puncture with a knife straight down to the heart, which I cut out and laid, steaming, on the floor. The damn thing just wouldn't quit! I worked careful like my father always did, pulling the skin back, splitting the legs – everything like you were supposed to. My brother kind of stood there, whistling, feeling pleased with himself for having killed a cow so dead.

Once an animal was cut up, you had to string the carcass from the ceiling for a couple days. For that purpose, we had tackle hanging from an old beam. Well, we tried best we could to hoist her up, but she was too heavy for us, so we had to go get my mother. She could hardly believe it. But we'd been taught to do everything else, so this wasn't so unusual as it seems now.

Maybe a week before the big day my father took us into the woods to get a Christmas tree for the house, the whole gang of us. He was like the Pied Piper with that ax of his. The question always was, which tree was the right tree? With that kind of choice, you always had a nice-looking tree, but it drove you crazy trying to guess which tree was best. Each one had its drawbacks: short limbs, a bare spot here, a brown patch there. The perfect tree, like the perfect anything, didn't exist. And the arguments we would have! With that many kids, somebody always has a separate idea about something. But my father didn't like too much talking, so pretty soon he'd say, "Quiet yourselves!" Then he'd hack down the one *he* liked, ignoring what we'd all been shouting. After it was down, we'd hitch a rope to the bottom end of it and drag it to the house, a dozen kids like a locomotive, all sticky and smelly with pine tar.

Decorating it was more than half the fun. There were a few ornaments that mother brought down from the attic – wooden angels and cows, things that got passed down through the family. Those went up first. Then we'd cut out white paper snowflakes and hang them around the tree. My oldest sister was the star maker. She'd make a big yellow one from tinfoil left over from packets of tobacco, and that would go on top. We'd make pretty chains for the tree by stringing together popcorn or, even better, cranberries or currants. There were candles, too – real candles – for lights, though you only lit them on Christmas Eve, what with the danger of fire. A fire on a farm was about the worst thing you could think of, especially in winter, when the pond was frozen.

While you were making decorations for the tree, you made decorations for yourself, too. The girls loved those salt beads, which took some concentration. First, you prepared some coloring. We had watercolors from our paint boxes and beet juice, and my mother had a row of food colorings. You poured maybe a cup of flour into a bowl, then added the dye, dribbling it in and mixing it. Then you kneaded it smooth, using butter from a big dish in the center of the table. You pinched off bits of dough and rolled them into beads, nice and round. You had to be sure they came out the same, or your necklace would look lopsided. Then you rolled the beads in a dish of salt – rock salt worked best. This gave the beads their sparkle. You could let them dry on the table, turning them over every few hours, or you could stick them on hat pins and set them by the stove. The last step was to string them and drape them – around your neck or around the tree. There was hardly a girl in school around Christmastime without a string of salt beads to show off.

On Christmas Eve, everybody would gather in the front parlor, and mother would read to us from an oak rocker with leather on the seat and a lattice back. Poems were popular in those days. She had a book of Christmas stories, too, so we always got one of those. The last thing was when we'd stand around the organ and she would play carols, pumping away at the foot pedals, turning the pages of the hymnal. Then we'd go to bed, thinking about Santa Claus, wondering what would happen that night and whether or not your stocking would be full. Maybe you'd hear the reindeer hoofbeats on the slate roof and maybe you wouldn't. I used to swear I heard Santa laugh one time, just before dawn, in the parlor. But you didn't dare sneak downstairs for a peek. Those were the times when sleeping three to a bed was lots of fun.

Christmas was a day for relatives and presents. My grandparents would arrive, with bundles, and usually some aunts and uncles. You'd have a big meal at midday, after opening the presents and trying out one or two of them. The girls each got a little bottle of Blue Waltz perfume every year. You'd get hats and gloves and sweaters, of course . . . not the sort of present to get you excited, but you needed that stuff. What you wanted was jewelry and games, like checkers, or anything else that was completely useless. The more useless the better.

There was a thing back then called the Travis sled, which had a front part and a back on runners, the two pieces connected by a board, and I remember getting one of them and being so excited we all had to rush up to the pasture to try it out. You'd ride half a dozen to a sled, which meant you never knew who, if anybody, was steering. It was a good way to knock your brains out, but you didn't worry about that kind of thing when you were young. You had your luck.

The big meal was big and then some. Meat – as much as you could imagine – maybe pork or beef, sometimes a turkey. If the men had been ice fishing up on the White River, you had fresh fish as well. And there was canned beans, sweet potatoes in maple syrup, squash, and apple sauce. There was always plenty of maple biscuits, too, or muffins. My father passed around his fizzy cider for the adults and the older children. My mother was one for the desserts, which meant you had your choice of pies and cakes. And after dinner there were stories – family stories, told over and over, and never said the same way twice.

It went on like this year after year, right through the 1930s. After that, things were never quite the same.

Christmas 1945

Walter Hard

It was all just as he remembered it:
The long village street with the irregular Green
About half-way down.
There were wreaths in windows and on doors,
And colored lights that would come to life at night.
Yes, and there was the big tree on the edge of the Green.
He was glad they had all these things back,
Just as they used to be before he had gone away.
He thought, as he drove along slowly,
Of all the strange places where he'd remembered that street.
The thought of it had often been the thing
That kept him going ahead –
Remembering to make himself forget.
He found so many packages
In the post office at Brayley's store,
That he had to make two trips to the pickup truck.
When he came back for the second lot
Old man Peters, who was sitting back of the stove,
Stuck his head out and said:
"Well Charlie, looks as though you'd bought out
A hul city store on your way back from discharge camp."
Charlie, who had almost forgotten the life of four years back,
Suddenly felt the home warmth in the old man's bantering tone.
After he had gone out, old man Peters shook his head.
"Can't see how they stood what they did.
I recollect, musta been 'bout a year ago now,
Charlie's father had a letter tellin' as how
The boy's outfit had got caught there in It'ly,
Been under shell fire fer a week, day and night.
Course Charlie spoke of dodgin' high explosives,
Makin' light of it.
I recollect he spoke of spendin' th' night
In a barn with the front blowed away."
Brayley sat with a far away look in his eyes.
Then he said:
"I recollect that letter.
I know it come just this time o' year.
The boy said he slep' in a manger."

*Walter Hard was one of
Vermont's most beloved
local poets, though his rep-
utation has not traveled
beyond the state's borders.
His numerous volumes of
poetry depict small-town
life in rural Vermont.*

49

from The Lone Winter

Anne Bosworth Greene

Greene moved to Vermont from Cape Cod "because the cars were suddenly under our noses." She wanted to live peacefully in the country and raise horses. Her diary, The Lone Winter, *published in 1923 to great acclaim, is among the finest examples of journal-keeping in Vermont's literary history.*

December 20.

Alas, another day gone in household industry, that demon which, when it seizes me, whirls me whither I would not go. Especially when work, in a good light by the window, is patiently waiting. Not a syllable did I produce, merely domestic glitterings. They are very nice, to be sure; I admire my two beaming kettles, and my stove edges like mirrors; I miss, pleasantly, the wreath of woodsy, licheny fragments that is apt to adorn the floor beside the big brass pot, the delightful but tippy receptacle in which I keep chunk-wood. Also I cooked up a week's supply of everything. Living alone, though one may try to have a balanced ration and all, one is casual about food. Balancing for one's own benefit seems so absurd ! . . . Cooking and shining up at once, however, is a triumph to the spirit and brings one out jolly at the end. It's a funny thing; I can, and do, with perfect cheer, spend no end of time on the animals' meals, meals served with muscle and strenuousness in exhilarating cold barns; but finessing around in a comfortable, warm house, dealing out little messes in plates and cups, fills me with depression.

In fact, I've been rather in the depths for days. Partly with headache, partly with an enormous sense of personal insufficiency because I can't, and never shall be able to, write in the tongue of the Highland Scot ! (I've been at Stevenson again.) An entirely unfair advantage on his part. There he had the heather – a monopoly of it; he had "the moorland where the whaups are calling"; *any* chance character of his could mention that the night was "pit-mirk" – and send shivers down your spine. . . . (Whereas a person nowadays has to say "pitch-dark," with no effect whatever. Not a shiver.) So I went drearily about my barn-yard jobs, quoting bitterly : ". . . and if he can hurt Ardshiel . . . If he can pluck the meat from my chieftain's table, and the bit toys out of his children's hands, he will gang singing hame to Glenure !" . . . Gang singing hame to Glenure ! – the purest poetry. And all because of that witching "gang" and "hame." . . . It's not *fair!*

But a strange meal, composed of dry bread, grapefruit, and "Bill Sewall's Story of T. R.," suddenly cured me. Chiefly the T. R. part of it; though abstinence has its virtues. . . . It has been a queer day. My morning went for little except a successful filling of the wastebasket, and this afternoon I rode six miles in a cold wind to call on a supposedly lonely family, and found them gaily entertaining company and not lonely in the least ! Sunday is the great calling day in the country; I should have remembered that. Then the work horses are at liberty

to have their "light harnessess" on, and farm-houses are alight with
sociability. As it was, Polly and I stayed but a short time and rode home
by moonlight, a thing to marvel at upon the snowy mountains. The sky
was filled with puffy clouds, among which the moon sailed, making
rainbow colors and throwing a flying light on silvered hills or darkened
valleys. The wind had fallen. Shadow-branches were thick on the road.
Once, in the woods, an owl screamed. Polly stopped and raised her head
at that; even Goliath, pausing beside us, lifted one fore foot, sniffed the
night air, and shivered. . . .

Our house, with its moon-lit roofs, looked sweeter than ever; in
my mind I lighted one or two of its windows. The evening star should
have been in its notch above the woods, but we were too late for that;
the whole blue sky was flashing with bold silver stars. . . . Inside the
barn, dusk and moonlight mingled so romantically that I unsaddled
without a lantern. It is fun to do that. You touch something warm and
wonder, "Is that your ear, Pip?" You feel delicately among straps,
finally, with a sense of triumph, stripping the bridle off without pulling
too much hair. I am used to uncinching without looking, though once I
mistook a hip for a wither, reached backward for the rear of the saddle,
and found I had firm grip of a handful of tail-bone! This frightened me
almost as much as it did Polly, who is not used to being grabbed in
wrong places and bolted into her stall with a snort of horror.

Next day I had to go to town. The "sleddin'" was harder than bones;
my sleigh bumped and jarred, and Polly, having lolled in a barn-yard
since the last trip, was none too gleg in the gaits. . . .

At last, under a pale-gray sky, over pale-gray roads, beside pale-
gray fields with bunches of sooty woods defining them, we jingled
deliberately home. It was lantern-time, and we had no lantern; this we
hoped no legal person would observe. Legal persons must have been at
their suppers, for no objections were encountered, and Polly, panting,
landed me at length in front of our shed. I tried to induce her to turn
the sleigh around, but it seemed to stick, and she lay down on the
shafts instead; she lay down about six times, first on one shaft and then
on the other. She did it gracefully; but I set my bag of eggs on a drift
and got out to help her (Polly loathes doing things in snow) and found
her fairly trembling with exertion and distaste. So I put her solicitously
to bed and backed it in myself. There were only Christmas-cards in that
sleigh, but it did seem heavy. I had to see-saw it.

December 29.
Christmas week, and my child is here, making everything gay with her
young ardors. So wonderful, to have *two* people dashing round the barn

with pitchforks! So brilliant an occasion, to be shoveling paths with the snow flying from a second, coöperative shovel! And above all it is thrilling to set out on the road with the rhythm of another horse step beside one. Polly feels it as much as I do, and foams with competition. Her knees fly nearly to her chin; and I hold her in for fear she will tire herself out. The Maharajah is delighted to have his little Missis here; his nose is perpetually over the edge of his box, looking for her; and when saddled he stands with a proud eye, waiting her word. . . .

On Christmas night a brilliant full moon rose, shining on the crust. It was twelve below zero. The rolling hills were like a silver sea. Moonlight gleamed on their tops and made shining paths. The belts of woods were black as ink. Riding home from a festive dinner at the Chickadee's, we gazed, though with teeth chattering; the horses galloped along the lighted roads, but even that exhilarating motion could not keep out the bite of the cold, and we turned gladly down the path to the barn. Before I could dismount, Polly quickly steered me to the watering-trough, with her little chivalrous air of "Oh, do let me save you the trouble of doing this later!" . . . But she bumped her nose on it! It was frozen hard; *and* the fence beside it shivered into bits!

Not a pony was to be found. They had had a kicking-bee by the fence, laid it flat, and departed. The crust was hard; they could go anywhere.

"Elizabeth – out at this hour!" I cried.

"And Donny – she'll freeze!" mourned Babs. The moon, though big, was still low above the hills; so we brought a lantern and scurried through the orchards (magically beautiful, with their purples against shadowy silver). There we discovered a stream of tracks on the hard crust.

It was dreadfully slippery on that crust; we slid along, holding the lantern at the tracks, and feeling every sword-sharp breath of air a stab in our hearts. . . . Would Elizabeth's little round furriness withstand this bitter night? So we hurried perilously over the slopes, where birch clumps sketched enchanting shadows, and the moon, soaring aloft, shone brightly down. The dark blue sky was thick with stars, the Milky Way solid with them; even the needless glory of the northern lights flared tongues of greenish fire upward behind the mountains. A night of celebration above, as well as on earth! and in the midst of such beauty our anxious quest seemed a bad dream. . . . It was Elizabeth's first Christmas! and we had brought her home a lump of sugar tied up with red ribbon. . . .

At the lane, tracks went in both directions, one stream into the dark woods. So we darted into a birchy hollow. Tracks were everywhere now, and round dig-places in the snow, where a hoof had scraped for food. We were both escorted by columns of steaming breath; "'Valleys where the people went about like smoking chimneys' – remember?" I panted, holding on to my nose, which seemed of a strange numbness. . . .

The bushy lane turned here, and in its shadows we perceived clusters of deeper blackness, from which a certain *breathing* quality arose . . . and then somebody very kindly sneezed!

"I'll get over the fence," whispered my child, with strategy learned of old, "and you go back to the turn and shoo 'em in when you hear 'em coming! I'll yell if I need you!"

Before I could even nod assentingly (as an obedient parent should) she was bobbing away. I dashed desperately back. If they got there before I did – and if the wrong pony was leading – all was lost! They would go tearing downhill into the woods. . . . If steady little black Fad had been with them, she would swerve into the home field; but alas! Fad was now far away, dragging a cart in Connecticut, and Ocean Wave, the swift and tireless, was leader of the gang. Mischief is the spice of Ocean's life. I could just *see* her dashing the whole crowd down into those shadowy depths, like the swine that dashed into the sea. Only it needs no especial devil to inspire my darling children; once get them in a mob, and out jump a dozen busy little devils ready for use – devils that a pony ordinarily keeps tucked away in the back side of his clever little head. And that pitch into the woods was a divine dash-place, geographically – and psychologically; being both a lovely downhill *and* the exact opposite of the direction in which they knew – *ad nauseam!* – they ought to go. How often had they galloped along that very land and shot piously in at the opening! And Shetlands, like people, can't bear being good *too* long.

Awaiting the onrush, I listened intently. All was still. The moon shone down through the trees, and lay in patterns on the frozen snow. Tiny sounds stole into the night stillness: a rustle, a crisping of crust, a frost-snap from a tree, the fritter of a dry beech-leaf; and, behind all these, the slow rise and fall of a murmur, a vast, slow murmur as from forgotten winds. . . . But from up the lane – silence. I grew anxious. Had they eluded my questing child and careered away? Should I stick to my post, or run and help?

Just then a crunching came to my ears; the crunching became a crashing, and round the corner of the birches dashed an agitated black mass, diving into the hollow, surging up over its crest, and roaring straight at me in full flight – a laneful of wildness! The woods for them! and midnight, and freedom, and frozen ears – hooray! Into the slivers of moonlight came a gallant blink of white; two silver knees flashing, an ink-black mane waving – Ocean Wave, simply going it!

"Hi!" I yelled, swinging my lantern in mad circles, and dancing furiously from one side of the lane to the other. Just as I caught the flash of Ocean's eye, and thought she was going straight through me, she swerved past – into the home field. A clot of others followed, galloping their best, swinging on desperate small legs around the sharp turn; then a single pony, shining golden against the shadow – Marigold; after her a string of slower yearlings, breathing loudly; then Queenie, a little black galloping blot on the moon-lit snow; and last – not to be hurried – the mare Thalma, at a laborious trot, with Elizabeth beside her. Finally, out of the darkness grew two attached but wrestling forms, about which expostulations hovered. "Stop, Superb!... Superb, don't be an ass!" and my child appeared, mightily restraining an agonized parent whose son had run on without her. Superb was knit into complete curves, her whole self a tense half-circle of suspense. Once safely in the field we let her go – and a chestnut streak shot into the valley, then up among the frisking mob of home-goers. We smiled at each other. Then our faces sobered.

"My! this cold bites!" muttered Babs.

"Got any nose?" I asked anxiously.

"Not much!" said she cheerfully, clasping it in a mittened hand. "You got any?"

In front of us were roofs and cuddling orchards; and to-night a single light shone out – that light I always longed to see. It made the whole picture; ... even if one knew it was candlesticks on a side-table under my child's portrait!... And the softness of the orchard-darks, above clear lines of silver fields – oh, dear! what a thing to draw – at twelve below zero, and ten o'clock at night! Things are always gorgeous just when it's impossible to get at them. ...

By the door stood a huddle of forms, meekly awaiting us. As we buttoned the door upon them, a sudden shock struck me.

"Where's Kindness?" I gasped.

"And Donlinna!" breathed Babs.

We had forgotten them completely! After a rueful glance at the freezing hills, we looked at each other and burst into shouts of mirth. Seizing the lantern, we set off, and nearly a mile from home came upon them standing disconsolately before a gray wayside barn, its front brilliant silver in the moonlight. Donlinna sprang to meet us.

"Bless you, Missises!" she wickered, running her nose into my coat-front.

"Why didn't you come home then, idiot?" I said, crossly, petting her; and started to put a halter on her. None of that! With a bound and a flourish she and her tributary pony were off, tails up, for home. Toiling in their wake, we had just one glimpse of them flying along the moon-lit lane. . . .

At exactly 11:15 by the kitchen clock we sat down to a Christmas supper. How marvelous the fire-heat felt; how joyfully the kettles steamed! Which was the greater luxury, to bask or to eat, we did not know. The candles gleamed among the holly; Boo-boo purred like a happy cello; and Goliath, on the hearth-rug, stretched out with a groan of content.

December 31.

We have put Kim in the hen-house, and Superb and Sunny with the yard ponies. Kim needed a yard of his own, and Superb needed society. She was growing very blue in the sole-company of her child, and spent her time peering over the fence toward the barn-yard, not exercising at all. There were kicking-bees at first, but things are now calming down, and the four new ponies form a sort of phalanx of defense, trailing around together. Kim is the one now suffering from solitude; but it won't hurt him. He must expect to be solitary. He was no further good to stir up the ponies, they were so used to him, – Superb is far more of a success in that line! – but his head is now perpetually over the bars, and he yearns for his ladies, kick him though they did. I passed him, the other day, and stopped to commiserate: "'Alone, alone, – all, all alone, – alone in a wide, wide' hen-house, Kimmie dear?" I inquired; and he wriggled his nostrils entreatingly. In mere desperation he dashes round his yard a great deal, which is very good for him; in the barn-yard, if he moved at all, some officious lady would rush up and bite him – and he would subside again into a sluggish heap. In winter he is really too gentle for his own good; all the ponies bully him; but in the spring, behold a dappled dragon, with green fire shooting from his eyes, issuing forth on two legs only, and bellowing as he comes! He tapped my shoulder once – slightly; but I have never walked in front of him since. As my expressive neighbors say, "It ain't safe!"

The Cultivation
of Christmas Trees

"You gotta be a jack-of-all-trades to work a small farm in Vermont," says Russell Maxwell, who has been farming a steep hillside near Rochester for thirty-six years. From the front porch of his nineteenth-century farmhouse the view is spectacular: row after row of mountain ridges, with a broad expanse of snowy fields in the valley below. "We got some cattle, some cows for milk. We got corn fields, an apple orchard, and a sugar bush. But, like a lot of us, I don't think this farm could pull its weight without the Christmas trees."

Like many of his neighbors Mr. Maxwell has a large stand of balsam fir, which he cultivates very closely. "Used to be farmers just let them grow, and they would go in there and take what they wanted come November. But that doesn't make for the best trees. People want a good tree nowadays, and you gotta take care of a tree."

"It's good conservation that pays," he says. "We don't cut anything that strikes our fancy. You follow the laws of nature. Give each tree space enough and light, and she'll do the rest.

"We aim for what's called 'sustained yield,' which means that you cut based on the average number of trees per acre and the annual growth rate," he says, his seventy-one-year-old face as full of grooves as a baked mudflat. A lump of tobacco puffs out one cheek. His flint gray eyes sparkle. "If you follow this plan carefully, you can take the same number of trees of about the same size every year from a given acreage. Works like a charm. And it goes on and on . . . indefinite."

By September, he has tagged the specially good trees for shipping out of state for stores, shopping malls, hotel lobbies, and outdoor display areas. These premium trees have been reserved long in advance by his special customers. Later, he cuts the ones ready for home use. "I get anywhere from five to seven loads cut by early December," he notes. "It pays the bills."

He planted Scotch pines first, but he found balsam fir easier to work with and more profitable. Throughout the year, he wanders his stand of Christmas trees with a knife in one hand – a machete, really, with a sharp, German-steel blade – and clippers in the other. "Nature sometimes likes a little help," he says. "And that's what I'm here for. I'm kind of a sculptor. You can thicken the tree, depending on where you cut. By shearing, you create that inverted cone effect people expect in a good Christmas tree."

Like any other kind of farming, fertilizers must be applied at

82

specific times in specific ways, "not too close to the trees or you burn the roots." While pesticides are not usually needed, weed killers come in handy, since weeds tend to choke balsam firs, sapping their nourishment. "You try to protect the trees from grosbeaks," he says, pointing to the little finches that flicker from limb to limb, "but it's not easy. They seem to find my buds kind of tasty."

Mr. Maxwell shows me a tree-tying machine, which takes the tree and thrusts them bottom-first into a plastic net, their limbs bound close, for easy shipping. "It's a damn good machine," he says. "You can pack them real close and not worry about damage. Each tree is individually wrapped, which is the way stores like them."

He creates his stand of premium trees by plucking wild seedlings from a nearby field, pulling them up by the roots, in August. He moves them to a transplant bed, where they spend two years, establishing a good root system. He figures the mortality rate for his trees, once they've spent two years in the transplant bed, is less than 12 percent. Once the tree has been planted in the final stand, it needs ten years in which to reach the height and fullness expected of a good commercial tree.

"What irks me," Mr. Maxwell says, "is that people imagine Christmas trees are a lazy man's crop. But it's year-round work. There's always something to be done. And once the fall hits, you work sunup to sundown. When Christmas itself finally comes, you sure breathe a sigh of relief. And, if the crop was a good one, you got reason to celebrate." Not everyone in Vermont resorts to commercial trees. In fact, those are largely grown for out-of-staters. There is still a continuing tradition here that might be called the "cut your own" state of mind. Most tree farmers are prepared for locals who insist on turning up with a saw or ax in hand. I think Charles Edward Crane, of Montpelier, puts it well: "It makes a fine prelude to the season, to sneak off quietly some bright December afternoon and go sleuthing for the perfect symmetrical specimen. It isn't good form any more to appropriate one: the Christmas etiquette is now to ask the privilege of hewing a tree in some farmer's pasture or woodlot (I heartily disapprove of poaching on any farmer's property in any respect whatever); and such is the holiday spirit that the permission is sure to be forthcoming. But a true gentleman, I think, should show himself equally generous and leave a token of his appreciation." J.P.

Christmas Cooking with Maple Syrup

Maple is the taste of Vermont, a natural way to sweeten and flavor desserts. This doesn't mean you can cook with what passes for maple syrup in most supermarkets! (Maple *flavoring* is not the same thing as the real syrup.) Vermont's maple syrup derives its special qualities from the soil and atmosphere, with the sharp drops and rises in temperature from late winter to early spring that make the running of the sap possible. Canadian syrup and New York State syrup vie with Vermont for pride of place, and each has its admirers. But nobody in Vermont thinks there is a race at all. The rich taste of Vermont syrup is like the nectar of the gods to the people who live here. Syrup is graded by color and delicacy from *A* to *C*. Reserve *A* and *B* for pancakes. For cooking, the crudest syrup is best: Grade *C*, which is dark and almost smoky.

The following popular recipes, all of which make generous use of maple syrup or maple sugar, have come down through generations of Vermont families. J.P.

MAPLE CREAM CANDY

2 cups maple sugar
½ cup thick cream
1 cup whole butternuts

Boil sugar and cream until it threads. Add butternuts, beat until creamy. Pour into 12-inch buttered cake pan, cut into a dozen small squares. Eat till sick.

MAPLE HARD SAUCE

⅓ cup butter
2 cups confectioner's sugar
2 tablespoons strong black coffee
3 tablespoons cream
3 tablespoons maple syrup

Cream butter, add remaining ingredients slowly, alternately. Beat constantly till fluffy. Spread generously on your wrist, lick well. (It's also good on gingerbread, on cookies, on ice cream and – for the real Vermonter – on homemade bread.)

MAPLE CUSTARD PIE

3 cups milk
3 eggs, separated
1 cup maple syrup
¼ cup sugar
1 tablespoon flour
¼ teaspoon salt
1 teaspoon vanilla
1 nine-inch pie shell

Scald milk, add yolks, well beaten, then mix syrup, sugar, flour, salt. Cook, stirring often, till it thickens slightly. Fold in beaten whites, vanilla. Pour into shell. Bake at 325° until firm. Makes one large pie. Not for calorie counters!

MAPLE MOUSSE

2 egg yolks
1 cup maple syrup
1 pint heavy cream
1 teaspoon vanilla

Cook beaten egg yolks and syrup in double boiler till thick, stirring often. Cool, fold in whipped cream, add vanilla. Freeze till firm. This makes six exquisite servings for a bedtime snack on Christmas night – the final touch to an elegantly sweetened season.

MAPLE GINGERBREAD

2 cups pastry flour
½ teaspoon salt
1 teaspoon soda
1 teaspoon ginger
1 egg
1 cup sour cream
1 cup maple syrup

Mix and sift dry ingredients, then beat egg, mix with sour cream, syrup. Combine mixtures, stir, turn into greased 9-inch cake pan. Bake 30 minutes at 350°. Add whipped cream or butter. Serves six hungry people. Nice for a snack after trying out that new sled on Christmas Day.

MAPLE CHRISTMAS COOKIES

½ cup butter
1 cup maple syrup
2 beaten eggs
½ cup milk
1 teaspoon vanilla
3 cups pastry flour
1 teaspoon baking powder
¼ teaspoon salt

Cream butter, syrup. Add eggs. Add milk and vanilla with flour mixed and sifted with baking powder, salt. Roll to ⅛ inch, use cookie cutter to shape into reindeer, stars, Santas, or Christmas trees. Makes 40 cookies with 2-inch diameter. Bake on greased tin at 350° for 8–10 minutes. Repeat as often as necessary. That is, whenever the cookie jar runs out.

MAPLE MORNING BISCUITS

1 cup maple sugar
2 cups flour
4 teaspoons baking powder
½ teaspoon salt
2 tablespoons shortening
¾ cup milk

Sift dry ingredients together, blend shortening. Add milk. Roll on floured board to ¾-inch tickness. Spread with maple sugar; roll out. Slice and bake in greased pan at 375° for 15 minutes. Expect about 20 biscuits. Great for Christmas morning while you're unwrapping presents.

MAPLE BUTTERNUT PUDDING

2 tablespoons sugar
¼ cup flour
¼ teaspoon salt
⅔ cup maple syrup
2 beaten eggs
1½ cup milk
1 tablespoon butter
1 teaspoon vanilla
⅓ cup chopped butternuts

Blend sugar, flour, salt. Add syrup, eggs. Heat in double boiler. Add milk, cook slowly. Stir often. When it becomes thick, add butter, vanilla. Beat thoroughly. Pour into glasses. Sprinkle with nuts. Serve chilled with whipped cream at the end of Christmas dinner. Serves six.

The Snow Angel
of Brattleboro

Snow sculpture is a favorite winter activity, one that reaches a state-of-the-art complexity during Dartmouth College's famous Winter Carnival. To a lesser extent, the University of Vermont and Middlebury College also practice the art during their respective carnivals. But long before sculpting in snow captivated the undergraduate mind, the art reached a state of near perfection during the Christmas holidays in Brattleboro.

It was December 1856, and a young citizen of Brattleboro, Larkin Goldsmith Mead, was so inspired by the Christmas spirit that his head filled with images of angels. He decided to sculpt the ultimate angel from ice and snow – an impromptu decision that lifted him to national fame as an artist.

Mead was one of nine children, the son of a well-to-do local lawyer. His mother was the sister of John Humphrey Noyes, who founded the well-known Oneida community in New York. At the age of nineteen, he began working as a clerk for Williston & Tyler, a hardware store. While waiting for customers to appear, he fiddled with a piece of Vermont marble on his lap, shaping a pig from the white stone. This neatly turned pig caught the eye of a wealthy visitor to Brattleboro's Hydroptic Institute – a place where people took a famous "water cure." Mead was sent by his patron to art school in New York City.

Two years later, on a Christmas visit to his hometown, he decided to craft an angel in snow. With a little help from his friends, Edward and Henry Burnham, he worked into the wee hours one night, in bitter cold. There was an iron foundry nearby, owned by the Burnham family, and they kept a fire burning. It was so cold outside that they took snow into the foundry itself, where they would partly melt it, then mold it to the imagined form. The angel gradually took shape – head, arms, wings. Mead did the sculpting, while Henry poured on water, coating the surface, giving it a hard enamel sheen.

It was morning by the time they were done. And the work was good. How good, they could hardly have guessed. When the town woke, they found the snow angel standing on a flat piece of land near the present high school – a dazzling image. A local paper recorded its impressions in no uncertain terms:

> Transcendentally beautiful stood the Snow Angel in the prismatic glow
> of the morning sun's reflection. The early risers and pedestrians about
> the town were amazed, when they drew near, to see a statue of such

exquisite contour and grace of form, with such delicate moldings and dimplings in details as to suggest the use of a chisel, and that only in a master hand.

Reports of the astonishing angel of ice spread quickly. Soon the *New York Tribune* and other national newspapers sent reporters. This was Vermont's Michelangelo. The face that this work of art was destined to melt somehow made the sculpture all the more precious. The story of Mead's angel soon spread to Europe and elsewhere. His angel had made him famous.

A patron of the arts from Cincinnati, Nicholas Longworth, quickly commissioned the young genius to reproduce the angel in Vermont marble, and he paid handsomely for this original work. Mead soon made further replicas, and one of them remains in Brattleboro, adorning the All Souls' Church. (The original later made its way to the Hall of Statuary in the Capitol in Washington.)

On the wings of his snow angel, Larkin Mead rose to permanent fame as a sculptor. Next to his famous angels, his most well known subject was Vermont's own Revolutionary War hero, Ethan Allen. He also did celebrated statues of George Washington and Abraham Lincoln. Later, he moved to Italy as a cultural attaché assigned to William Dean Howells, the novelist, who was an American consul in Florence. Mead died there, far from Vermont, in 1910, having married an Italian woman and made a permanent home in the town where Michelangelo did some of his finest work.   J.P.

The Light at
Scromfit House:
A Christmas Story

Jay Parini

It was a long time ago in a small town in western Vermont called
Barrington. The countryside around Barrington consisted mostly of
dairy farms, with a few apple orchards and sugar bushes thrown in for
good measure. The town itself was tiny, having only one general store,
one bank, a one-room schoolhouse (for all grades), two churches, and a
post office.

The town clustered in a narrow valley, about thirty or forty houses
made of wood. Each was beautifully maintained, with white clapboard
siding so white that, in winter, the houses almost disappeared against
the backdrop of snow. Add to this the predominance of white birches,
which could be seen everywhere in Barrington, and this could be
counted among the whitest towns in the United States of America.

Only one house was not white, the large brick house on the hill
next to the cemetery, called Scromfit House. The dark red bricks it was
made of, and the immense size and peculiarity of its shape, caused it to
stand out strangely in this otherwise modest town. The children of
Barrington thought it must surely be a ghost house, since it had many
turrets and queer little windows and extensions and perhaps three or
four stories full of bedrooms that couldn't possibly be occupied by
living human beings.

The owner of Scromfit House was Mr. Eleazar Scromfit, a wealthy
lawyer who had retired many years ago after his wife had died. Mr.
Scromfit lived in the big house with his two grandchildren, Lizzy and
Matthew Bean, who had been left in his care by their father, Colonel
Sanford Bean, who was fighting a war in a faraway country. (It was well
known that Mr. Scromfit did not approve of Colonel Bean and had
begged his daughter not to marry him. He had not even attended the
wedding.) The children's mother, Ellen Scromfit Bean, had died two
years before of a tropical fever (she was buried in the graveyard beside
Scromfit House), and the children had no one to look after them while
their father was away except their uncle, who did not like children
very much.

The townsfolk of Barrington worried about what might be going
on in the big red house. For one thing, Mr. Scromfit had never been
considered a pleasant man – not in many years. He did, however, belong

to the town's Musical Society; that is, until his daughter died. He had a strong baritone voice, and he liked nothing better than when the Musical Society performed a concert of Christmas music. This concert was usually followed by a party at Scromfit House, where cookies and cider were served and presents were handed out to the choir. But that stopped abruptly when Ellen died.

Now the people of Barrington wondered if the Bean children were being treated properly. Were they well fed? It was known that a local woman, Mrs. Higgertig, came every afternoon to prepare an evening meal and, once a week, to clean the house from top to bottom. This was said to be a good sign. It was also noticed that a teacher, a Miss Doob, was brought in three mornings a week to give the children lessons, although it was considered odd that Mr. Scromfit refused to let his granddaughter and grandson attend the local schoolhouse, which had been good enough for generations of Barrington children. Indeed, a former governor of Vermont had graduated from the Barrington school, as had several prominent citizens of Barrington, including Mr. Scromfit himself! And why had he chosen Miss Clarissa Doob as tutor? For a start, Miss Doob was very old herself, almost as old as Grandfather Scromfit. She lived alone in a small cottage at the edge of town and was considered strange.

The townsfolk rarely got a glimpse of Matthew and Lizzy except on Sundays, when they attended the Congregational Church with their grandfather, who sat between them in the front pew and insisted upon perfect behavior: no talking, no sneezing or coughing, no chewing gum, no giggling or passing notes back and forth. Mr. Scromfit told the children they could move their mouths to the hymns, but they must not actually sing. It was not polite for children to sing in church, he said. More important, he told them they must not under any circumstances socialize with the other children of the church, whom he referred to as "ragamuffins" and "hooligans."

"They have terrible manners . . . dreadful," he sputtered. "If I catch you speaking to any of them, you're in trouble with me. And you know what that means."

The three of them made quite a sight in church: Mr. Scromfit with his huge head shaped like a watermelon with wild, white hair that brushed against his stiff collar and stuck out at the sides, and the children — Matthew was seven, Lizzy six — with their navy blue matching sailor suits and shiny shoes. They sat in the front pew, near the pulpit, in full view of the congregation, who whispered rude remarks about Mr. Scromfit behind his back.

Matthew and Lizzy were by nature obedient. They were also quite unhappy living in Scromfit House with their old grandfather. If it were not for each other's company, there is no telling what might have happened to them.

Now that Christmas was approaching, they became even sadder. Last Christmas, Santa Claus had brought them nothing at all: not even a piece of candy, a red apple, or a small bag of nuts. Lizzy remembered that horrible day only too well. She and Matthew had come down the dark stairwell of Scromfit House from their bedrooms at dawn on Christmas Day, hoping to find lots of presents under the large spruce tree that Grandfather Scromfit had ordered cut from his own property for his grandchildren. He had told them that Santa rewarded good children with presents and punished bad children with nasty surprises. They never dreamed that Santa would punish them, since they had been especially good that year considering the fact that they had been left alone in Vermont with an old grandfather. It had also not been long since their mother's death.

But that morning, instead of presents, they found a bucket of coal under the tree, and their stockings were full of coal dust. A message from Santa was scrawled on a piece of paper and lodged under a piece of coal. "Dear Matthew and Lizzy. You have not eaten your porridge. You have refused green vegetables. No presents for you this year. Sorry." It was signed "S. C."

They noticed that their grandfather was already awake, standing in the doorway in his long dressing gown and rubbing his long crinkly fingers.

"Oh, Grandfather, it's so sad," Lizzy said. "Santa has left us nothing but coal."

Matthew looked grimly at his grandfather and said nothing. He was determined that next Christmas would, no matter what, be a better one for them both.

That day, he bundled up and walked, alone, into the little graveyard beside Scromfit House. His mother's tombstone was covered with fresh snow, but he wiped it clean. He wanted to see her name in clear, bold letters: Ellen Scromfit Bean. He put his lips to the stone and kissed it. And he prayed that, next Christmas, his mother would make sure that little Lizzy got more than coal dust in her stocking. About himself, he did not care. (Although he would have loved a drum or a bugle or a box of ginger cookies. What boy wouldn't?)

One thing that Matthew couldn't understand was why his father never wrote them letters from the war, as he had promised. "Matthew," he had said on the night before his departure, "You will get a letter from me every week. Your grandfather will read it to you." In fact, Matthew had been a good reader for some time, and he looked forward to getting letters from his father. He knew that Lizzy, too, would love to read them, since she had recently learned the alphabet from Miss Doob.

Every day, at lunchtime, Mr. Gringly, the postman, trod up the long icy hill to Scromfit House, and Grandfather Scromfit rushed down the steps – no matter what the weather – to greet him. He invariably brought an armful of letters into the house, which he quickly took into his study – a room that was strictly off-limits to Matthew and Lizzy.

"I have important papers in my study," Grandfather Scromfit told the children. "You must never go in there. It is my private room. If I ever catch you in there, you know what will happen."

"Has a letter come from my father?" Matthew used to ask, almost every day.

"Nothing from him," Grandfather Scromfit would say, turning quickly aside.

Now Matthew had pretty much abandoned hope that his father would write. He supposed that fighting a war in a faraway land was tricky business, and that his father simply had no time to waste on letters to young children. But he vowed that, when he was a grown man, he would always take time to write letters to his children, if he should have any.

Still, life at Scromfit House was not as bad as it might have been. Grandfather Scromfit did not actually beat the children or shut them in their rooms. He did not scream at them or demand much of them. In fact, they were usually left to their own devices, except that they were bound to appear at meals and go to bed when the clock struck seven. Of course, they had to attend church and do whatever lessons were set by their teacher, Miss Doob, but none of this was especially difficult. If anything, they would have preferred to have *more* lessons and to go to church *more* often.

It was also a fact that Miss Doob liked the Bean children and tried to make their lives more pleasant. She asked Mr. Scromfit if she might take them into town occasionally for what she called "educational walks." She would teach them about the natural world, explaining how the valley had been formed millions of years ago by glaciers. She would talk to them about the development of towns and take them into the bank and post office. She would do this and that, she said. Mr. Scromfit didn't seem to care, so long as Miss Doob reported regularly to him about their activities. She agreed to this quite happily, and the children noticed that Miss Doob spent a good deal of time reporting to Mr. Scromfit on their activities.

The excursions into town became a wonderful ritual, one that immediately followed every successful morning of reading, writing, and arithmetic. They might stop at the local drugstore for a fizzy ice-cream soda at the counter or stop into the tobacco store for a peppermint stick or some licorice. Now that Christmas was almost upon them, they would peer into the brightly lit store windows or dawdle on the public green beneath the gaily decorated pine tree beside the church. On the last day before the school holidays, Miss Doob let them stand outside the one-room schoolhouse and listen while the children of Barrington sang carols like "Silent Night" and "Hark the Herald Angels Sing."

One day, Lizzy said to Miss Doob, "I wish you were my grandmother, Miss Doob."

Miss Doob became red in the ears. "Enough of that talk, Lizzy Bean."

"My grandfather doesn't love us, you know," Lizzy said.

"That's not true," Miss Doob said. "I know that he loves you. He talks about you all the time. It's just that he has been very sad lately. Perhaps you should spend more time with him."

Lizzy listened carefully and said she would try, but she was afraid of her grandfather and didn't think she really would. She, like her brother, had decided long ago that Grandfather Scromfit disliked them, so they almost never spoke to him directly.

Meanwhile, with Christmas approaching, Grandfather Scromfit seemed to grow ever more silent. Scromfit House became a dreary place to live.

"Can we have a Christmas tree, Grandfather?" Lizzy asked one evening.

He seemed quite startled that she had spoken to him. "What for?"

"Santa might want to bring us presents this year. We have been eating lots of porridge and green vegetables, haven't we?"

"Have you?"

"We have," she insisted.

Grandfather Scromfit looked at her very hard, but he did not reply. The children quickly guessed that, this year, no tree would be cut from the property. They would have to pretend that Christmas didn't exist.

It was on Christmas Eve that Matthew Bean had his big dream. He dreamed that his mother had come back to life, that she had emerged suddenly in a whirl of snow, and that she was standing beneath his bedroom window, beckoning, dressed in white. Still asleep, he walked down the chilly stairwell, opened the back door of Scromfit House, and wandered out into the freezing night air.

It was below zero, and the snow was falling fast, swirling in funnels like little tornadoes of white. The large, sloping garden looked like an endless frozen desert. By the old willow tree, which hung down with ice crystals on its bare limbs, a strange light was shining about five feet off the ground. As he stared intently at this light, he knew in his heart it was his mother, and he ran toward her through a steep snowdrift, falling at the base of the tree.

He looked up at the glowing circle, but he could not see her face.

"Mama!" he cried. "I can't see you, Mama!"

Her voice came, clear and pure. "Your grandfather loves you, Matthew, but he doesn't know how to show it."

"No, he doesn't, Mama," Matthew said. "He hates us. He hates me and he hates Lizzy."

"Listen to what I say, darling," she said. "He loves you. If you remember that, everything will be all right. Ask him to sing for you." With that, her voice trailed off in a swirl of wind.

Matthew woke suddenly, shivering beside the tree. The light was gone. Thinking he had been dreaming, he ran into the house, as cold as he had ever been in his life, with tears still burning on his cheeks.

When he got inside, he shook the snow from his pajamas and wiped his bare feet, which had turned almost blue with cold. He stood by the wood stove, which was still throwing heat though it was now long past midnight.

When he felt a little better, he tiptoed back into the hallway on his way to bed, passing his grandfather's study. The door was closed, as ever, but the light was on. He could see it shimmer in the crack beneath the door. He paused, wondering what to do. If his grandfather was in there, perhaps he should knock. Perhaps he should listen to his mother and ask him to sing, right then and there.

He knocked, gently, but it was his sister's voice that answered.

He pushed open the door. "Lizzy! What are you doing?"

She was seated at Grandfather Scromfit's big desk. Beside her, on the floor, was a small trunk full of letters. "Look," she said, putting a stack of envelopes into Matthew's hand. They were addressed to him and Lizzy, and they were mostly unopened.

The children huddled in their grandfather's leather chair and began to read. One by one, they opened and read each letter aloud. It was nearly dawn by the time they had finished.

Suddenly, heavy footsteps pounded down the hall! It was Grandfather Scromfit!

Matthew had forgotten to close the door, and the children saw the huge watermelon head charging toward them, their grandfather's eyes glaring like coals.

Matthew ducked beneath the desk, terrified. But Lizzy remained calmly in the chair, watching Grandfather Scromfit as he rushed past the study without even looking in. The children heard the kitchen door open and slam shut with the wind.

"Let's go," Lizzy said, taking Matthew's hand. She seemed to know exactly what was happening.

They stood at the kitchen window and peered through the frozen windowpane. Grandfather Scromfit, his white hair whiter than the snow, knelt by the ancient willow. A light was shining like a small flame beside the trunk.

"He's speaking to Mama," said Lizzy.

Matthew could hardly believe it. "Have *you* been talking to Mama tonight?"

She nodded. "She told me about the letters. She said that Grandfather has been hiding them from us, but that we shouldn't be angry with him. He can't help himself when he's mean. But everything will be different now. Just wait and see."

Grandfather Scromfit knelt in the snow for a very long time. When he came in, Lizzy flicked on the light.

"Grandfather, you must be *freezing*!" She led him to a chair and folded a thick carpet around his legs. His feet were soaking wet, so she dried them with a towel.

"Would you like some tea?" Matthew asked. "I'll boil the water for you."

Grandfather Scromfit nodded.

When he had drunk some tea and stopped shivering, he reached out for Lizzy and Matthew, pulling them close to him. He had never done this before.

"Why did you keep the letters from us, Grandfather?" Lizzy asked, without a trace of anger in her voice.

"I was being selfish . . . or stupid. I don't know why I did that, Lizzy. But I'm sorry. People do things that make no sense when they're angry and sad."

Grandfather Scromfit began to cry now, and Lizzy gave him a dry cloth for his eyes. Suddenly, the red light of dawn broke over the mountains, and the room began to glow.

"Will you sing for us, Grandfather?" Matthew asked. "It's Christmas morning, isn't it? We would like it very much if you would sing."

Grandfather Scromfit looked skeptical.

"Please, Grandfather," Lizzy insisted.

Grandfather Scromfit smiled, his face crinkling like tinfoil, and without hesitation sang "It Came Upon a Midnight Clear." His voice was rich and deep, and the old pots and pans on the walls vibrated with the booming sound. The glasses in the cupboard tinkled.

"I wonder if you would like to come down into the cellar with me," he said, having finished the song.

Lizzy and Matthew agreed to go. The cellar had been strictly off-limits, like the study, and they were curious about what was down there.

Without explaining a thing, he led them down the dusty stairs, carrying a bright lantern. All the while he was humming "Joy to the World."

The cellar, it turned out, was full of toys. There was a long sled, a doll, several horns and drums, and a game of checkers. The toys were covered with dust and very old.

"These were your mother's. But now they can be yours," Grandfather Scromfit said. "Merry Christmas!" And he kissed them both on the cheeks, hard, as he had never done before.

The children took the toys, one by one, up into the kitchen, where they dusted them off. The sled had a broken runner, but Grandfather Scromfit promised to set to work on it that very day. "I can fix it," he said. "I'm sure I can." The doll, though its hair needed a good wash, was in decent shape. The drums and bugles worked just fine.

"And I will teach you both how to play checkers," Grandfather Scromfit announced in a proud voice. "I'm a very hard man to beat, I shall warn you right now."

"Can we call Miss Doob?" Lizzy asked.

"Miss Doob?" Grandfather Scromfit asked, a bit puzzled by the request.

"She will be all alone on Christmas Day," Matthew added.

Grandfather beamed. "I will invite her myself . . . for Christmas dinner. What a good idea! Let's get dressed, and we can go together to her house to invite her."

Nobody was more surprised, of course, than Miss Doob, who welcomed them in her nightgown with an astonished face. And it just so happened that Miss Doob had a gigantic turkey in her icebox. That afternoon, they sat about the table at Scromfit House and sang Christmas songs and ate turkey till they were almost sick. It was at the end of the meal that Grandfather Scromfit produced a telegram from his jacket pocket. It was from Colonel Bean. "Dear Matthew and Lizzy," it read. "Arrive Christmas Day. 4 P.M. Home for good!"

At that very moment, the clock in the hall struck four, and there was a sharp rap on the kitchen door. It was Colonel Bean, a suitcase in one hand, a bag of presents in the other! As the children hugged him and hugged him, a small light whirled in the snow, like a saucer, but it was seen by no one except Grandfather Scromfit, who happened to be looking out the window with his arm around Miss Doob.

A Green Valley Christmas

John R. Hilliard

Hilliard, a lifelong Vermont enthusiast, was an occasional contributor to numerous little Vermont magazines in the early 1920s.

Who would not see Green Valley at Christmas?

We know what her summers are like for we have journeyed there and breathed the enchantment of her mountains, meadows, and streams; we have seen the moon-silvered peace of her tiny lake; we have climbed up the rugged paths of her hillsides; we have slept among the ferns in her cool hollows; we have quaffed refreshing draughts from her bubbling roadside spring; we have obtained deep contentment in the sequestered solitude of the place; we have found satisfaction in observing the honest faces and homely ways of her people; and we have doubted if there be another locality more like what Heaven must be than this garden spot in God's great universe.

We have lingered on into an autumn when over the valley there rested a brooding serenity disturbed only by the scream of the crow, and the sound of dropping nuts in the still woods. Then we saw a scarlet magnificence, broken by orange and umber and the green of spruce and hemlock, sweep across the hillsides and swamps, continuing up the mountain heights, setting the peaks ablaze in glory, under the silent, violet-blue sky.

There was the exhilaration of the crisp, starlit October nights, the witchery of hazy day-breaks, the fascination of majestic sunsets, riotous in incredible color, the repose of the loitering sunset, the joy of the garnered harvest.

There were corn-huskings and barn dances and other rustic merrymakings, accompanied by pans of snowy popcorn, and mugs of cider fresh and sweet from the press. But when the first storm swept down from the western hills, and the wind roared and moaned through the trees whose branches were fast becoming leafless, when ragged clouds sped portentously over our heads, then we deemed it well not to put to the proof our quaking forebodings; we hasted away as fast as our feet would carry us to escape the more rigorous blasts of a late Vermont autumn.

We were scarcely ensconced in the cozy luxury of our town apartment, however, before we felt again the call to the country – to Green Valley.

It is always so with those who once find this sheltered, secluded dale among the Vermont hills. The people who go there for a week or a month, in summer, return again and again as the years roll around so that they come to regard themselves, and to be regarded, as belonging to the valley.

Let a Green Valley man drive over to a neighboring town, or indulge in a trip to a neighboring state. If he chances to meet a fellow townsman instantly a glad light shines in his face, and his heart beats more buoyantly because of the handclasp and hearty greeting of a man from home.

Once a Green Valley resident journeyed down to a Connecticut city. Possessing an amiable, neighborly disposition, he introduced himself to his seat companion in a trolley car. In due time and with natural pride he informed him that he hailed from Vermont. The city-dweller looked up interested.

"I am a Vermonter, by birth," said he, "but my parents left the state when I was a very young child."

"Where did you live?" asked the visitor, with his characteristic eagerness.

"Our home was in Montpelier," answered the man, "but I was born in a town called Green Valley."

"Green Valley!" exclaimed the country-man, his countenance illumined with the light of love. "Green Valley! You born in Green Valley! Bless my heart! Why, man, I was born in Green Valley myself, and it has been my home all the sixty years of my life. Please God I may die there! Say," he continued after pausing a moment to regain his breath, and to gaze at his new acquaintance, "when I first set eyes on you I knew you were not like the ordinary run of men around here – not but they're all right, every one of them, but, you see, there's a stamp on a Green Valley native that won't come off, and he can be detected at a glance." Again he paused, but only for an instant. "And you were born in Green Valley! Why, my dear sir, there's no other place like it in all the world! Come up to Vermont and see for yourself; and be sure to make your home with me while you're there."

The result was that the gentleman travelled up into the Vermont mountains, saw his native town, cried out in ecstasy, and swore his perpetual allegiance. He sought out the house in which he was born, and purchased it, intending to become a summer resident; but when he retired from business he sold his town house and spent the remainder of his years in the hamlet of his nativity.

Thus Green Valley weaves her spell and her charm is never broken. Her people come and go. New faces appear within her borders. Her children are suddenly transformed to men and women. But Green Valley herself never changes. Her mountains round about continue steadfast. In friendliness they look down upon the valley dweller. They even speak to some, so human do they grow as, in varying moods, lights and shadows play across them. Sometimes when their summits are veiled in cloud masses, or bathed in the purple light of the twilight glow, their call sounds loud and clear.

"Return, my children," they cry. "We love you well. We will build you up. We will help you to be strong."

So we heard again the call of Green Valley, and the yearning grew within us to see it at Christmas.

Our first thought was to engage rooms in the village hotel but, as though divining our desires, there came a letter from Cousin Esther, asking us to spend ten days with her and Cousin Ephraim on the farm. They live a mile out of the village on a narrow, picturesque road, bordered by stone walls and rail fences. Their farmhouse is one of the oldest in town, having been erected near the close of the Revolutionary War, but, like the houses in the Acadian village of Evangeline, it was strongly built with "frame of oak and of chestnut." It stands snugly sheltered near the foot of Cedar Mountain, and hospitality gleams from every window and clapboard and shingle.

It was four days until Christmas when, in afternoon, we alighted at the little station in the adjoining town of Blandford. There, standing on the narrow platform, was Cousin Ephraim so enveloped in a huge fur coat and cap that we did not recognize him until he seized our hands in hearty greeting.

Soon we were packed into the long red sleigh and to the lively tune of jangling bells and the prancing hoofs of the big, gray farm horses, we started on our ten-mile ride to Green Valley. With soap-stones at our feet, bricks in our hands, and fur robes wrapped closely and comfortably around us what minded we the sting in the frosty air?

Strangely unfamiliar was the road! Where in leafy days of summer were maples and elms and oaks now arose only their bare brown trunks and leafless branches. No sound came from the muffled brooks under their covering of snow and ice. The cliffs, our delight in summer days, when dripping with tiny rivulets, were noiseless and almost hidden from view by thousands of icicles, gleaming in myriads of colors. The knolls where cattle fed sparkled in icy splendor. Lying over the whole valley was a deep, thick shroud of snow, and there hovered a solemn silence.

As we rode northward the outlines of Green Valley came into view – the irregular broken fences, half buried in snow; the lonely farmhouses; the grist mill; the lake all frozen and white; the harness shop; and, then, before we caught sight of the village itself, the square tower of the old white church loomed on the winter landscape. How our hearts burned within us as we saw it all again! Over beyond us rose Monument Mountain, calm, majestic, magnificent, in the glow of the afternoon sunset. The clouds resting over her, which when we left Blandford appeared gray and ominous, were transformed, as if by magic, to crimson and gold and green, while across the valley all the eastern white peaks were bathed in colors, delicate and ethereal – lavendar, rose, and pink. Never before had we beheld a picture of such dazzling gorgeousness. Even the snow at our feet was suffused with warm color. We held our breath in mute amazement. Then before the glory faded, and before darkness swept over the valley, we found ourselves on the porch of Cousin Esther's home, wrapped in her motherly arms.

The next day Cousin Ephraim remarked, as he came from the barn after finishing the forenoon chores, "There's a storm a-brewin'. I see a ring around the moon last night, an' it had one star in it. That's a sign fer certin that we'll git a storm within a day or so. Guess there's no doubt but we'll have a white Christmas. Wal! let her come! There's nothin' more entertainin' than a good snow storm."

Sure enough, a haze was forming over the sky and, listening, we heard the "Mountains roar" – an unpropitious omen. Ere afternoon was far advanced the flakes began to fall, slowly at first, as a fine mist, then gradually increasing. An early twilight fell. The air was filled with the tossing, whirling elements. The wind arose. It moaned and soughed through the spruce trees in the yard. The branches of the big willow overhanging the house creaked and groaned on the roof. Fierce gusts whistled around the corner. The shutters rattled. But inside all was warm and a cheery contentment pervaded the long, low rooms. Cousin Ephraim added chunk after chunk to the crackling stove fire, while we ate popcorn and butternuts, meanwhile laughing and listening to his tales concerning Christmas when he was a boy. Ah, no wind can ever drive the glowing lustre of that winter night from our memories.

In the morning the storm was not abated. Snow filled the air with blinding fury. Fences were completely buried and deep drifts blocked the roadway. It was a wonderful sight – that swirling mass of snow, blotting out the landscape, and almost isolating us from the world.

Towards noon we saw the first sleigh pass the house. The horse wallowed and floundered through the difficult drifts, the sleigh tipped dangerously to one side and then the other, and we watched in breathless interest until it disappeared over the brow of the hill. Not until mid-afternoon did the second one struggle by, and then Cousin Esther, jumping to her feet, hastened to the window, exclaiming, "Another team! Well folks are out a real lot to-day, aren't they?" How we shouted! And Cousin Esther laughed with us! But that was characteristic of her optimism. We learned, during that winter visit, why she had never been lonely on her remote Vermont farm.

"There'll be no mail to-night," she said, as dusk approached. "Abner will not attempt to make the route to-day. He couldn't possibly do it."

Abner was the rural mail-carrier, a happy-go-lucky fellow who stopped at each farmhouse, dispensing and gathering news. He was as welcome as the birds in June.

"Then why shouldn't I go to the village for it?" urged Cousin Jim, the happy thought bursting suddenly upon him. "There's nothing I'd like better than to breast a December storm in Vermont and, truly, I need the exercise."

Cousin Esther only half demurred. The arrival of the mail was the one diurnal break in the monotonous existence of the long, hard winter months. Accordingly Cousin Jim lost no time in donning moccasins and furs, preparatory to setting out upon his enterprise.

Ah, but it was cold as he plunged into the swarming storm, with the wind biting at his nose and fingers. No trace of the tracks made by the two straggling teams during the afternoon was visible. He stepped into a deep drift and was immersed to the waist line. He pulled himself out, but repeated the procedure over and over. Shortly his whole being tingled with exhilaration, for a gale is enticing. It is rare sport to brace against it, combatting it, while it beats upon one, striking mercilessly. He passed the cheese factory. How fantastic it looked, shrouded in white, in the fast-gathering gloom! Its roof reminded him of one of Cousin Esther's Christmas cakes which she had piled high with frosting. He smacked his lips in anticipation, and plodded across the bridge on to the village road.

Dim lights shone from the scattered houses through windows whose panes were half-concealed with snow. In the village an occasional street lamp had been lighted, but its faint twinkle was scarcely perceptible through the mass of spinning snowflakes. Now and then he met a villager, with lantern in hand, toiling through the street, for the sidewalks were impassable. As they met they exchanged greetings in genuine country fashion.

Suddenly, as he rounded the corner, it seemed as if he must run up against Bob Stanley, his companion of Green Valley summers, or hear the voice of old Keziah call out, "Hello, Jack Washington," as she had been wont to do in former days; but Bob was far away in Buffalo, working at his profession, and Keziah's worn hands had been meekly folded since his summer visit. For a moment a sensation of desolation and intense longing swept over him and then, ere he realized the fact, he had opened the post-office door and was standing beside the high, round stove.

"Merry Christmas!" he shouted, and the postmaster, recognizing his voice, bounded over the counter in his haste to welcome him. The postmaster and Jim were friends of long standing. His impetuous greeting and their lively conversation alone repaid Jim for the effort he had taken. He filled his pockets and piled his arms with mail — packages, bundles, newspapers, letters, Christmas cards – and, light-hearted, he entered upon the last lap of his excursion.

Cousins Esther and Ephraim were waiting for him in keen expectation.

"Yes, the cousins are coming from Bennington and Richmond," she cried, joyously, after opening her letters. "What a Christmas we're going to have!" Her eyes sparkled with excitement, and Cousin Ephraim danced a jig on the parlor carpet.

"What say to a game of euchre?" he called exuberantly, as his feet came down with a rattling crash. We, catching his enthusiasm, sprang merrily to our places about the card table.

What a game we had! How we laughed and shouted, gloating over our successes, ridiculing and deriding the losers! Peering back to that winter night, into the low, old-fashioned parlor, warmed by the sheet-iron stove, and lighted with a curious hanging lamp, once more the kind friends gathered round that table seem to be sitting there again – Cousin Ephraim boisterously slapping the cards down on the marble top, Cousin Esther looking on in mild surprise, the guests with countenances wreathed in smiles – and over and above all the gladness and love of the Christmas season.

Oh, snows and winds of that long ago! Oh, cousins in that mountain home! Never again will there be the same elation and delight as crowded into our hearts that Christmas week in Green Valley.

At ten o'clock the game was called off and into the kitchen, one by one we marched for the tallow candles which were to guide us up the narrow stairway to our chambers. There stood Cousin Ephraim before us, in his hand a mammoth piece of mince pie, which he was devouring greedily. On the table by his side lay the remnants of the pie but, although he urged us to fall to and finish it, we did not yield to his solicitation, preferring to find our land of dreams unmolested by raging monsters.

The wind was "going down" when we sank into our feather beds, albeit occasionally a fitful gust shook the rafters. Then our bedsteads rocked, and we drew the homemade quilts Cousin Esther's mother had fashioned closer round our heads, but with less and less frequency came the blasts until quiet reigned in our world.

The morning that dawned was brilliant and sparkling. Cold was the air and crisp the snow under the clear blue sky. White fields glistened in the radiance, and the hills stood out like mountains of ice upon a frozen sea. It was the day before Christmas.

During the morning hours the business of breaking roads and shoveling paths occupied every hand. Over the hilltop came the slow-moving snow plough drawn by patient horses. Eagerly we watched its advance along the road until it reached the driveway leading to Cousin Ephraim's house. Onward it came into the yard making a passage up to the very doorstone, and then to the barn where the frost-covered animals were enveloped in blankets, while the teamsters trudged into the roomy kitchen amid a great stamping of feet and slapping of hands benumbed with cold.

Steaming cups of hot coffee, together with a big pan of doughnuts, were passed around, and as the visitors drank and ate they related weird tales of the havoc the storm had wrought. A woman in Jason Hollow had lost her way and, being overcome with cold and fatigue, lay in the snow for hours. Marsh Walker had gone with his family to Chippendale and the roads becoming pathless, he had been forced to remain there. Men, shoveling out drifts and noticing no stir about his place, made investigations. They cared for the stock which had been without food and water for a day and a night. Old Mrs. Hanks had had a stroke, and no doctor could get to her until life was extinct. Telegraph lines were down. Trains into Blandford were long overdue. The stage from Dover had not been through.

We listened in incredulity. So protected were we in Cousin Ephraim's warm house, little thought had there been of inconvenience or suffering. But instantly Cousin Esther was alert. Packing a basket full of bread and cake and pies, she impressed one of the hired men into service, and dispatched him down the narrow road leading to the Hankses. Later in the day Cousin Esther herself, not too busy with her household tasks, visited the home from whence the Christmas angel had borne a soul to Heaven.

All day long a bustle of preparation was going on in the farmhouse kitchen. Ann Lake, an accommodating neighbor, came over to "help." She chattered like a magpie while she washed dishes and swept, but she turned off work like a steam-engine, Cousin Esther asserted.

Cousin Ephraim set up the Christmas tree in a corner of the parlor. Red and white candles were fastened here and there to be lighted at the proper time. These with the tinsel and bright-colored streamers made it a festive sight. Bewildering packages hung from the lower, stronger boughs, and on the floor, around and beneath the spruce branches, were placed the larger ones.

Oh, it was good to stand in that parlor in its festal decoration with the sun pouring in through every window, and the breath of the kitchen, odorous with the scent of baking viands, permeating every corner of the house!

On the evening train were to come the cousins from Bennington and Richmond, and again Cousin Ephraim, in the long red sleigh, journeyed to Blandford. Late it was and cold when he reached home, for trains were not yet running on schedule, and drifts, being deep, the horses made slow progress. The stars were out, and the moonlight was so brilliant that the outlines of the trees lay shadowed on the snow. Cousin Esther sat by the window, an animated participant in our conversation, at the same time listening for sounds indicating the travelers' approach. Long before the party crossed the bridge, she announced the fact that they would soon arrive, for her quick ear had caught the sound of bells, and, opening wide her door, laughter and shouts filling the night air, heralded the coming guests.

What a welcome they received! Everybody shook hands and hugged everybody else; old dog Bruce set up a tremendous barking as if he, too, sensed the importance of the occasion; and, for a time, pandemonium reigned.

Finally when quiet was partially restored, and the guests had been divested of hoods and caps and coats and mittens, they drew around the stove to engage themselves in the business of renewing old acquaintance. Then, again, what a Babel! Everybody talked and it appeared that each one desired to make himself heard above everybody else. Cousin Ephraim was the leader of the group, his voice resounding over the others as he described the perilous ride of the evening in language ridiculous yet convincing. His auditors shrieked in convulsive merriment.

Meanwhile, Cousin Esther busied herself in preparing a lunch and, when all had eaten, the grandfather's clock which had ticked away the years of many a life leisurely tolled the hour. Cousin Ephraim stopped abruptly in his narrative. Turning to Cousin Esther, he exclaimed, "Well! well! it's time you tucked us in our beds. We mustn't lose our beauty sleep."

As we snuggled into our blankets the white hills shone across the sleeping valley under the glow of numberless stars, and the peace of Christmas settled over the homestead.

We were awakened long before daylight by Cousin Ephraim kindling the fire, followed by Cousin Esther's call, and shouts of "Merry Christmas!" from every room. The uproar continued until the hour for breakfast when we assembled 'round the table, partaking ravenously of buckwheat cakes swimming in maple syrup, great plates of doughnuts, and huge cups of delicious coffee. Not a great deal of ceremony was connected with the meal, but a superabundance of hilarity atoned for any lack of formality.

How comfortable it was in that low-beamed kitchen, for we were eating there, the dining-table having been "set" the day before, by Ann Lake, in readiness for the Christmas dinner.

It was impossible to look out upon the Christmas world because a thick coating of frost covered the window panes but, by-and-by,

when we stood upon the porch, an entrancing vision met our eyes. All
the mountain peaks were like pyramids of sculptured marble, long
reaches of silver fields gleamed in the sunlight, the little brook flowing
through the yard gurgled tunefully under its fetters of ice, and the
branches of the kingly spruces in the farthest corner of the lawn bent
under their weight of snow. Nothing could have been more fitting for
Christmas Day.

Later we were summoned to the parlor. In sheer ecstasy of joy we
clasped our hands, and a murmur of delight ran through the company as
they beheld the scene. The room had been darkened. Lighted candles
were glowing from the piano, the mantel, and every available space; and
the tree, covered with dancing tapers, made an enchanting picture.

Cousin Esther sat by her old-fashioned piano and softly she began
to play that ancient Welsh melody to which the words "'Tis Christmas
Day" have been set. A hush fell over the room as she and Cousin
Ephraim began to sing:

> "Oh, what mean these songs they're singing?
> 'Tis Christmas Day.

One by one, the others took up the words:

> "Oh, what mean these bells they're ringing?
> 'Tis Christmas Day."

and thus they continued to the end:

> "Loud we raise our happy voices,
> All His world in Him rejoices!
> 'Tis Christmas Day."

The faces of the old cousins shone with the light of happiness. They
loved to sing, and the Christmas carols made a special appeal to them.

Then they began:

> "I saw three ships come sailing in
> On Christmas Day, on Christmas Day;
> I saw three ships come sailing in
> On Christmas Day in the morning."

Not all of us were familiar with the words; but Cousin Ephraim sang
the many stanzas. Then they passed on to that delightful old carol sung
to music, harmonized by Sir John Stanier:

> "God rest you merry, gentlemen!
> Let nothing you dismay,
> Remember Christ, our Savior,
> Was born on Christmas Day,
> To save us all from Satan's power,
> When we were gone astray."

The voices rang out joyfully and the chorus was sung with triumphant power:

"*O tidings of comfort and joy,*
Comfort and joy,
"*O tidings of comfort and joy.*"

Cousin Esther's fingers wandered up and down the keyboard until she played the opening notes of that dignified twelfth-century carol, so universally beloved:

"*Draw nigh, draw nigh, Immanuel,*
And ransom captive Israel,
That mourns in lonely exile here,
Until the Son of God appear."

Again we all joined lustily in this chorus:

"*Rejoice! rejoice! Immanuel*
Has come to thee, O Israel."

Over and over the refrain was repeated until, at Cousin Ephraim's request, we united in Luther's fine old Cradle Hymn, written for his own child:

"*Away in a manger, no crib for his bed,*
The little Lord Jesus lay down his sweet head,"

and again, in the beautiful hymn sung to the strains of an ancient Breton melody:

"*O'er the cradle of a King*
Hear the song the angels sing!
In excelsis gloria."

Never before had these carols produced the answering chord they awoke that morning. They repressed us and calmed us, those melodies so strangely vibrant with emotion, showing us a side of Cousin Ephraim and Cousin Esther we had hardly known before, and filling our own hearts with adoration and worship.

From one familiar tune to another they turned until Cousin Esther struck up "Home Again," and the walls rung with the exultant notes of the old-time favorite:

"*Home again, home again,*
From a foreign shore!
And oh! it fills my soul with joy
To be at home once more."

Truly, we were "home again," and fortunate to be on that lovely farm among those kind and virtuous friends.

Suddenly, Cousin Esther sprang to her feet, declaring the packages must be opened and, without more ado, we proceeded to disrobe the tree. What fun it was to open the bundles! and what surprises they held for us! Now we burst into peals of laughter at a joke some one had perpetrated; again, only with difficulty could we find words expressive of our gratitude for an article that hitherto we had thought of only with yearning. All in all, our hearts overflowed with tenderness and thankfulness.

And then the dinner! Can one ever forget it – the table stretched to its greatest length; the centerpiece of holly branches; the oysters and turkey and chicken pie; the pies and pudding and Christmas cake; the oranges, nuts, and candies; and Cousin Ephraim's voice: "Father, for these and all thy mercies, for the love of home and friends, for the gift of Thy Son born to us this day, we thank Thee."

What a Christmas Day that was! From early morn till even-song its hours were gracious and endearing. But slowly it slipped away. Try though we would to restrain it, the shadows gathered and fell across the valley, the moon arose again, the stars came out. With it went our laughter and our songs, but its memories have not faded, nor shall they as long as one of that dear company is left in the world alive.

The attending week continued in long-remembered pleasure. In the village there were skating parties and sociables and dances. A Christmas tree and concert were functions in the church, and the young minister and his wife kept "open house" for their parishioners and friends. There were sleigh rides and card parties and a Grange supper. All the week long Green Valley buzzed in gayety, and then it settled back into its customary tranquility.

To this day our blood tingles with the stimulation of that country Christmas season. We cannot return to it, nor can it come again to us. We know, however, that those days have not entirely passed, that Green Valley varies never. We know that as the winters come and go the same blanket of snow covers the sloping fields, and that the same frost crystals scintillate the frozen crust. Down on the mill pond the ice grows thick and thicker, and boys and girls glide over its smooth surface. The brooklet flowing through Cousin Ephraim's yard gurgles among channels of ice, and over the ghostly hills and woods countless stars look down from the canopy of heaven. Out of the twilight and gathering darkness the homestead lights still radiate, and at Christmas time, the bell from the church steeple sends up and down the valley its glad message of "Peace on Earth, Good Will to Men."

Good-by and Keep Cold

Robert Frost

This saying good-by on the edge of the dark
And the cold to an orchard so young in the bark
Reminds me of all that can happen to harm
An orchard away at the end of the farm
All winter, cut off by a hill from the house.
I don't want it girdled by rabbit and mouse,
I don't want it dreamily nibbled for browse
By deer, and I don't want it budded by grouse.
(If certain it wouldn't be idle to call
I'd summon grouse, rabbit, and deer to the wall

And warn them away with a stick for a gun.)
I don't want it stirred by the heat of the sun.
(We made it secure against being, I hope,
By setting it out on a northerly slope.)
No orchard's the worse for the wintriest storm;
But one thing about it, it mustn't get warm.
"How often already you've had to be told,
Keep cold, young orchard. Good-by and keep cold.
Dread fifty above more than fifty below."
I have to be gone for a season or so.
My business awhile is with different trees,
Less carefully nurtured, less fruitful than these,
And such as is done to their wood with an ax –
Maples and birches and tamaracks.
I wish I could promise to lie in the night
And think of an orchard's arboreal plight
When slowly (and nobody comes with a light)
Its heart sinks lower under the sod.
But something has to be left to God.

Frost was Vermont's most celebrated poet. The state's official poet laureate, he lived on a farm in Ripton.

List of Photographs

Designed by Matthew Bartholomew and Douglass Scott
at WGBH Design, Boston
Production coordinated by Nan Nagy
Type set in Monotype Centaur and Arrighi
by Michael and Winifred Bixler, Skaneateles, New York
The paper is 100# Celesta dull by Westvaco
Printed by Federated Litho, Providence, Rhode Island
Bound by A. Horowitz & Sons, Fairfield, New Jersey